While every precaution has been taken in the preparation of this book, the publisher assumes no responsibility for errors or omissions, or for damages resulting from the use of the information contained herein.

DOG HEALTHY GUIDE FOR A HAPPY DOG LIFESTYLE: CARE, ORGANIC FOOD, DIET, NUTRITION, GROOMING, EXERCISE, WALKING & OBEDIENCE TRAINING

First edition. July 25, 2017.

Copyright © 2017 C. Lexington.

ISBN: 978-1386538059

Written by C. Lexington.

My Favorite Quote

THE ONLY CREATURES that are evolved enough to convey pure love are dogs and infants.—Johnny Depp

Way 1: Undertanding Dog Food Ingredients

Understanding the ingredients of your dog's food items is a must for the dog lovers or dog owners. Whenever you feed the dog with different kinds of food items, you should always read the label and understand the contents about the dog feed types that are being used in such commercial preparations. You should understand the ingredients while buying food for your dog and also know what to look for.

Feed items include dry and fresh food. The fresh dog food that is prepared in homes generally consists of ingredients like freshly cut chicken pieces in addition to the cranberry juices, blue-green algae, etc.

• • ∽ • •

ALSO FEED PASTA, BEET pulp, soy bean oil, calcium carbonate, wheat middlings, magnesium oxide, iron sulphate, copper sulphatezinc oxide, choline chloride, etc. These are often the ingredients in case of a vegetarian based diet offered to dogs.

• • ∽ • •

Raw egg, chicken, beef, mutton, fish, quail etc. are often the preferred ingredients in case of dog diets that are prepared on the basis of the non-vegetarian items. Taurine is one of the essential ingredients for the dog's nutrition. Like wise, in the case of dogs feed with frozen fish items, the vitamin called thiamine needs to be supplemented as an ingredient.

Many premium type of dog food preparations contain essential fatty acids, carbohydrates with adequate fiber contents, vitamins like A, D, E and B complex vitamins.

Furthermore, minerals like zinc, is an essential ingredient for skin health status and calcium, which is an essential ingredient for bone growth, tonicity of muscles. They should be enriched in these food items. However, the cost of those food preparations are comparatively more expensive than the food preparations with general ingredients. Though it may be better for your dog's health.

TIP:

Your Dog loves treats like biscuits, and similar things. Prior to taking the steps in training your dog, you should make sure to prepare some treats as rewards and whenever your dog is able to follow your command. Make certain that the treats you have prepared is really something he loves. If you reward him with these tasty treats he really knows that he has done something right.

Your dog's behavior, health, happiness, well being and longetivity totally depend on what you feed your dog. Although there are a variety of dog foods available in the market, natural dog foods are considered to be the best for a dog's health. These Natural dog food plays an important role in the overall development of your dog. Your dog will definitely stay healthy and fine if natural dog foods are given on a regular basis.

Natural dog food recipes are not difficult. If you want to strengthen the immune system of your dog then natural dog food recipes are a must.

Your dog will no longer suffer from any kind of allergies or fleas. Natural dog food recipes are much better than processed pet food recipes. Lack of natural dog food may give rise to coat and skin problems and other serious health problems.

You can always take the help of internet if you want more knowledge about natural dog food recipes. There are a number of websites that provide natural dog food recipes.
Natural dog food recipes are a major source of energy and hence it is essential to feed your dog with these foods. A recent survey has found that many are taking the help of books to prepare their own natural dog food.

Dogs not only survive but thrive on these natural dog food recipes. This natural dog food recipe is safe and healthy for your dog

Akita Style Rice and Lamb: The ingredients of this dog food recipe are lamb, brown rice, broccoli, potatoes, carrots and kombi.

WAY 2: DOGS NEED DIFFERENT Diets At Different Ages

Dogs need different diets at different ages.

This happens to be true. As an example, the little dog desires milk as the major food item while an adult dog may need meat or chicken as well as the boiled egg and milk. So dependent on the age factor, the diet schedule varies actually for the dogs like every other species. Puppies need bigger amounts of protein, fat and carbs than an adult dogs. Additionally, puppies require more frequent feeding schedules in a day, unlike an adult dog.

The movement based needs of diet are way more in the case of puppies, since they're frequently more active than the adult dogs. Elder dogs need constrained protein but the protein should be simply digestible and simply absorbed in the body. The diet schedule should have sufficient supply of water for them.

Feeding aged dogs too much protein may eventually lead straight to over burden to the renal structures and in the end the dog may finish up damaging filters in the kidney.

This really is true particularly when the immune response of these dogs is compromised due to several factors. In a similar way, the aged dogs need less food just because the movements of the adult dogs are highly limited and thus, they should spend a limited of energy.

FEMALE DOGS IN THE pregnancy stage do not need to be fed too much. Feeding too much will result in some discomfort. Especially the pregnant animal and the nursing animal require special sort of foods that deliver a well-balanced sort of nourishment with correct reinforcement of minerals and vitamins. The nursing dog must be fed with enough amounts of calcium, too.

Way 3: A Healthy Dog Diet

Choosing a healthy dog diet can be confusing and difficult if you let it. Your dog's diet is the most basic way to keep your pet healthy and happy for the years to come. A dog diet that is terrific for your neighbor's dog may not be exactly what your pet needs.

The first step when considering your dog's diet, is to talk to your veterinarian.

Find a reputable brand of dog food to be the main component of your dog's diet. It is not impossible to stumble across a high-quality dog food that you have never heard of, but a well-known and prominent manufacturer provides an amount of safety and security about the decision to feed your dog a healthy diet. If your dog is older and shows signs of aging, consider a dog diet that is specially formulated for senior dogs. You may want to keep this in mind when selecting your dog's diet.

Activity level and weight are other factors to consider when making the decision of what to feed your dog. If your dog is extremely active or overweight, you may need to pick a type of dog diet that accommodates such situations. Your dog's diet should consist of a high-quality food specially designed to meet your pet's dietary needs. Giving your pet too many supplements in the dog's diet can lead to a lower quality of health.

Always consult your vet for advice on what to feed your dog. Your dog's diet will fuel his health, so choose your dog's diet wisely. Finding the right diet for your pet will promote good health and allow your dog to thrive.

WAY 4: HOMEMADE DIETS

Home made diets are significant in the dog feeding. Many a times, the commercial diets are composed of foodstuffs that have synthetic coloring agents and flavoring agents that are damaging to the dog's body.

Home made food stuffs have the guarantee of freshness in the preparation in stark contrast to the ready made commercial items. The chemicals added in the commercial foods would possibly not be the acceptable ones to the dogs from the health viewpoint. Even in the event of renal sicknesses in dogs, the home made diets could be made with ground meat, bits of bread, calcium carbonate, boiled eggs and so on.

SUCH CASES MAY GET simply treated once the dog food is modified from the commercial sort of food to the home made foodstuffs. Frequently the home made food is prepared utilizing the freezing procedures to destroy the germs or by adding grape seed extracts to provide adequate anti-oxidants to the home made foods.

Food grade vinegar is also added in numerous times to the protein pieces prepared in a fresh demeanour. All of these can be improved with vitamin additions that are generally available in fruit essences, fish oil and so on.

Cranberry juice, fish, bananas and protein are prepared in a top notch demeanour and no additives are added during the preparing of these types of food. The dog becomes more active after the consuming of such nutritious food.

Way 5: Vitamin And Mineral Supplements

MINERAL AND VITAMIN additions are the most vital parts in any dog's feeding.

If there's a balance in the mineral and vitamin additions, then the animal will have a good life and thus, the protection isn't compromised in an unwelcome way. This basically means that there the dog will be more illness resistance against diverse illnesses.

Owners of pets should really know that vitamins A, D, E, and K are the fat-soluble vitamins and others are water-soluble vitamins. Vitamins like thiamine, pyridoxine and cyanocobalamin are significant for the functions of nerve system. Deficit of vitamin A leads to night blindness and skin abrasions and inadequacy of vitamin D leads to the softening and weakening of the bones.

AMONG THESE, VITAMIN A toxicities may happen if you feed them in unjustifiable amounts, like vitamin D. Therefore, give good care while you are using these vitamins.

Cod liver oil from selected fishes has more vitamin A and is generally a good feed for dogs. All dogs may not need additions of minerals or vitamins to live comfortably, but it is critical for their future. If they get sick or if they are aged or if they are really young without correct feeding, supplementations are needed for the upkeep of their health status.

But one has to follow the directions of vet in this context. If the dogs are fed with fish in frozen conditions, then they could be suffering continually from vitamin B1 inadequacy and therefore, such dogs have to be given in particular B1. Sloppy supplementations of minerals may well lead to sicknesses and therefore, vets always have to be consulted on the reinforcement of minerals or vitamins.

Minerals like calcium, magnesium, zinc, manganese, iron, copper and so on. Are given more stress as well as sodium and potassium. Zinc is related to peel health and potassium is related to the muscle health and calcium with phosphorus is related to the bone health.

. . ✺ . .

NONETHELESS IF YOU feed the dog with chicken, meat or mutton along with veggies, synthesised reinforcement of mineral or vitamin capsules could be highly reduced but additions must be thought of when you are unable to maintain a well balanced nourishment.

Also make sure to provide proper water and food. Providing these healthy foods for dogs does not just make sure that he is in a good shape, but it also makes sure that his senses are sharp which in turn helps when it comes to training the dog. Give him very nutritious food and fresh water all the time.

Way 6: Dry vs. Canned Food

These types of food materials are different with different grades of liking by the dogs. Dogs like dry foods only if they are tasty only and however, on comparison, the dogs prefer only the canned food items. Reason for such preference by the dogs is that in case of canned food items, the moisture is about seventy to eighty per cent but in case of dry food, it is only about ten per cent.

However, if you view it in terms of nutrients, often the dry food contains nearly ninety per cent nutrients whereas the canned food items contain only less per cent of nutrients and most of the times. It is only soy products that are structured so well to look like meat pieces.

Hence, to make up the nutritional balance in the body systems, the dog has to eat more amounts of canned food materials than the dry food materials. Hence, just compare the cost factor related to this feature by you. Many dry food items are soybean and rice based.

Now some dry food items are based on corn. Sometimes, beef based or chicken based food items come in the cans along with mineral and vitamin supplements suited for the upkeep of the dog's health status. Larger dogs that weigh more than thirty pounds need to be fed with semi moist food items or dry food items in most of the occasions.

This is to satisfy the food receptors in the stomach. This is due to the fact that the larger dogs need to eat plenty of moist food or the canned food items to satisfy these criteria. But it may not be practically possible in these larger dogs. The small sized dogs may have a satisfactory level of nutrients if fed even the moist food items.

THE CALORIFIC DENSITY of the dry food shouldn't be forgotten.

Enriched and improved dry dog foods are preferable to the food that is non-enriched.

Way 7: Cost Of Dog Food

If you are feeding your dogs with different kinds of food items make sure to watch the prize tag closely!

The cost of dog feed is one factor that is most important in the case of feeding of dogs with different kinds of food items. Yes. This is true. The cost factor needs to be looked into in various perspectives during the preparation of the food items, required for the balanced feeding of dogs with proper vitamin and mineral supplementations in the food.

Cost will not always matter much because the dog's value is being assessed in terms of companionship and the happiness derived from the dog to the dog owner. Though the cost of the food items is comparatively more, many dog owners don't mind much due to the increased benefits derived from their dogs in terms of protection, guiding, etc.

Selection of ingredients for the home made food needs to be however based on the quality factor. Even when the quality is more, general persons may seek some cheaper items only. Recommended nutrient contents may be obtained from the national nutrient academies in all nations and this will provide guidelines.

One can correlate the cost factor with items available in their own country. Generally, the commercial food items are expensive especially the ones that use the modern technologies of food preparation like oven-baking, sterilization of cans, air drying or freeze drying of contents etc.

CANNED ITEMS COST MORE than dry foods. Nevertheless the price of these feeding items do rely on what type of food item you are going to utilize for your dogs. Food sensitivities have to be monitored during use of different foods.

Today, almost all of the dog food labels have discussed their cost and quality on the package itself so that you can make an informed decision. You can also use the internet to do more research in relation to the quality and the specific ingredients that are contained in a specific dog food label or a specific dog food product.

Way 8: Dog Food Allergies Causes & Remedies

Food Allergies

Dogs can develop allergies or food sensitivities at any point during their lives. Often, dogs eat the same type of food for years, so their diet may be overlooked. The most common problem causing foods include:

- Soy products
- Beef
- Chicken
- Corn
- Wheat
- Pork
- Milk
- Whey
- Eggs
- Fish
- Lamb
- Chemical Preservatives
- Artificial Sugars

Symptoms of Food Allergies often include:

- Itchy Skin
- Ear Inflammations
- Ear Scratching
- Frequent Licking or Biting of Paws
- Anal Itching
- Face Rubbing
- Head Shaking
- Loss of Appetite
- Coughing

BETWEEN 15% TO 20% of all dogs in the US do suffer from nasty food allergies. As in humans, allergies may manifest in different kinds producing varied symptoms in your dog. It is important to knowing the signs of the allergy suffering to bring your dog a faster relief and a happier life. As with any dog related medical problem, always make sure to consult your vet if you do suspect any problem.

Remedy:

Once food allergies have been determined to be the cause of your dog's symptoms, eliminating the potential allergens from your pet's diet is the first course of action. Begin by excluding foods which are known instigators (see list above).

Look for either a commercial product which contains ingredients your dog has not eaten before or prepare home-made food for your dog consisting of two parts starch to one part protein. Suggested protein alternatives include duck, salmon, venison, or rabbit. Potatoes are suggested as an alternative starch. All ingredients should be served boiled and fed in normal proportions to your dog's regular diet.

Once prepared, the food can be individually packaged, frozen, and then used as needed. Home cooked diets are generally nutritionally incomplete and should only be used temporarily during the test period.

One item at a time, begin adding ingredients present in your dog's former food to his new food. If symptoms reappear, the food allergen should be easily identified. During the test period, make certain your dog eats only the new food.

Eliminate treats, dog bones, table scraps, rawhide, chews, vitamins, etc. Once the offending food has been identified, look for a commercial food which does not contain that ingredient.

Atopic Dermatitis

Atopic dermatitis, or canine atopic dermatitis, is an allergic skin disease generally caused by an immune hypersensitivity to environmental substances such as mold spores or dust mites. Indications your dog has this sensitivity generally present themselves by the age of two. Food and flea allergies, as well as parasitic infections, should be ruled out first as their symptoms are similar to atopic dermatitis.

Symptoms of Atopic Dermatitis include:

- Excessive Grooming
- Licking or Chewing of the Paws, Stomach, or between the Toes
- Change of Stomach Skin Color to an Irritated Red
- Ears which are Red or Hot to the Touch

Remedy:

- Skin allergy testing can be conducted by your veterinarian to determine your dog's specific allergy.

FLEA ALLERGY:

Caused by the saliva secreted by the flea, a flea allergy is the most common form of dog allergy. Sometimes the bite of a single flea may cause your dog to launch into fits of self-chewing and biting lasting for five to seven days.

Symptoms of Flea Allergy Include Severe Biting & Chewing of:

- The Tail and Surrounding Area
- Stomach
- Inside hind legs

Remedy:
A skin test can be performed to confirm your dog is allergic to flea saliva. Once a flea allergy has been confirmed, a strict control regimen should be initiated. Flea control products are safer now than they once were with options ranging from topical solutions to pills, shampoos and sprays. Garlic and Brewers Yeast have also been touted to keep fleas away as have weekly topical applications of lavender and eucalyptus oils. However these solutions have not been scientifically confirmed.

Whatever remedy you choose, consult your veterinarian first. Overly strong flea killing preparations may cause your dog more harm than good. Additionally, regular dog grooming (through your dog's coat and down to the skin) will help find and eliminate fleas and flea droppings.

INHALANT ALLERGY:

Inhalant allergies are substances in the environment which cause your dog's immune system to react, releasing antibodies containing histamines, serotonin, and leukotrienes. Pollens from trees, grass, ragweed as well as mold spores, chemicals, dust mites and wood chips in pet bedding may cause your dog substantial discomfort.

One clue to diagnosing this allergy is timing. Is your dog's allergy seasonal or year round? If you know to what your dog is allergic, avoidance is the best remedy. To help mitigate possible allergens, use dehumidifiers to reduce mold, air conditioners during pollen season, air cleaners with HEPA filters for dust and pollen residue, and vacuum frequently.

Inhalant Allergy Symptoms Include:

- Biting and scratching at the body
- Red or Irritated ear flaps which are hot to the touch
- Head shaking
- Rubbing the face
- Severe scratching or biting of the flank, groin, paws and armpit regions

REMEDY:

Providing your dog relief may come in the form of a cool bath with colloidal oatmeal, aloe vera, eucalyptus, or a medicated shampoo. However these will only provide your dog temporary relief and will need to be repeated frequently.

Omega 3 and Omega 6 fatty acids are natural anti-inflammatory agents which have proven successful in approximately 20% of dogs tested. Omega 3 fatty acids are found in fish oils such as Cod and Omega 6 fatty acids come from plants containing gamma-linolenic acid - such as evening primrose. Antihistamines have also proven effective in dogs with allergies with one short-term effect being lethargy or tiredness.

Corticosteriods (steroids) are substances which interfere with the function of the immune system and reduce itching by reducing the inflammation. They also affect all the organs in your dog's body and should be used under medical supervision for short periods of time or in small doses.

Blood tests and intradermal skin testing can also be performed to judge specific reactions to allergens.

CONTACT ALLERGIES:

Contact allergies are the least common of dog allergies. Items such as flea collars, grass, shampoos, plants, chemicals, and wood chips may cause allergic reactions. By eliminating the irritant, symptoms should disappear.

If you think your dog may suffer from allergies, keep a journal. Make notes as to the symptoms, their severity, and when they occur. This will help your veterinarian pinpoint the problem and help your dog achieve a speedier recovery.

WAY 9: IDENTIFYING Food Allergies

Food sensitivities are something that's tough to identify unless one is acutely aware of the baseline info with respect to this sort of allergy. The primary signs of food sensitivities in dogs include the facial itching, limb gnawing, belly itching, re-occurring ear diseases or skin illnesses.

Since the dogs consume lot of prepared food materials including diverse types of proteins, fillers, coloring agents and more ; in the commercial food materials, the occurrences of food sensitivities are rather more than one can imagine.

.. ⁖ ..

ALLERGIC DISPLAYS TYPICALLY involve the skin or the gastro abdominal tract. If you come across your dog itching after the supply of express food materials, then suspect a diet allergy in this animal. Nonetheless, conditions like fungal complaints have to be eliminated generally before the conclusion of itching as an indication of a diet allergy.

There are several recorded occurrences of allergies to corn or to wheat. Nonetheless the diet allergies differ from dog to dog. Read the labels obviously before feeding your dogs with pet food materials.

Too much coloured food materials could be evaded since they may result in allergies. Dietary allergies are sometimes interlinked to the hyper active behaviour spotted in dogs.

Added colours, additives, and a high-fat diet may cause such dietary allergies in the dogs and therefore. You need to be careful in providing new sorts of food or diets to your dog and tightly observe the dog for any sign of allergy.

There are numerous occasions that dietary allergies could be diagnosed in a dog, but the dog could have other issues like pancreatitis. To disqualify the diet allergies, observe your dogs each time you feed your dog.

Also look for some reasons to link the indicators with the food given and watch for the specific encountered signs.

Then check with your vet.

Way 10: How Much Quantities Should I Feed My Dog

Many people will give different types of answers based on their experience with their dogs. However, the scientific facts related to the feeding aspects in case of dogs need to be given emphasis during the feeding activities maintained in case of dogs.

Usually the puppies should not be separated before they are eight weeks old. However, some times the orphaned puppies may exist. Usually about five percent of the body weight may be taken as criteria for the quantity of food to be given to the puppies. However, the amount that is consumed by the dog varies with size of the dogs also.

NONETHELESS, THE RULE of feeding the baby dog goes till you see perceivable fullness of the stomach to a respectable degree.

If you're going on feeding the animal without giving focus to the animal's stomach appearance, then the little puppy may experience some sorts of digestive upsets and the diarrhoea may happen. This will cause many troubles to the owner as well as the little puppy.

Unlike adult dogs, the puppies have to be fed with constrained amounts of food but in more frequencies.

Nevertheless once the age advances, the amount might be increased to a point but the frequency of feeding is sometimes reduced in numerous occasions. A dog on a raw diet may consume only 2 to 4 % of their body weight.

Just observe closely the feeding pattern of the dog and the body condition of the animal. If the dog becomes overweight, just reduce the amount of food and if the dog becomes thin, then have a rise in the feeding items.

As discussed earlier, puppies and teen dogs eat more than the adult dogs. Similarly the geriatric dog eats less than the adult dog thanks to the reduced movements of the dog.

Way 11: How Often Should I Feed My Pooch

This often becomes an important question asked by many dog lovers and dog owners. If it is a puppy within age of the first six weeks, the puppies need to be given milk at the rate of five to seven times per day. The puppy will make some sound if it wants to feed in general.

However, the feeding frequency may be reduced when the dog becomes six to eight weeks old. By the time the dog assumes the age of four weeks, it may start taking of some solid food. Hence, mix the solid food with water in majority and feed your puppy once or twice in the beginning and if the dog develops some diarrhea, then delay the feeding.

Most of the times, it is due to trial and error but taking some basic steps in feeding, so you need to watch out. The feeding frequency may be changed to two to three times after the assumption of age of eight weeks. However, if the dog is seen hungry craving for food, then provide food once than the estimated numbers. This varies with different breeds of dogs.

THE PUPPY WILL BE TEETHING around 3 months to 6 months of age. This is why you should avoid feeding a puppy at this age too many times.

Try to restrict the feeding to 2 times per day only, but the balanced type of nutrition needs to be provided to the puppy of this age group to avoid the deficiency based symptoms in puppies.

From 6 months to 1 year, try using specific puppy food that is available at stores or dog boutiques. However, from the first year onwards, you can give your dog the regular adult dog food as well.

However, when the dog becomes a senior dog, make sure to restrict the frequency of feeding during the day since the movements of such elder dogs are highly reduced due to their age.

Way 12: Boredom And How To Add Variety

DULLNESS AND VARIETY are always inter connected in the event of dog misbehaving.

Boredom experienced dogs may have different types of behavioral patterns. For example, some dogs will be seen barking continuously and some may be engaged always in some digging activities.

There are many ways to get your dog out of its boredom activities. Many toys are available which simulated duck, dog, rodent etc.

These may be kept inside the crate and in particular, puppies love these items. A buster cube with multiple treats may be placed in the dog's shelter and the animal soon understands on how to roll the buster cube to get the treats it prefers. A Buster Cube is an ingenious toy use for simulating and activating your dog during play and feed time. Instead of placing the food monotonously in one place, change the place of feeding suddenly.

SUCH ACTIONS WILL BE very beneficial for removing the boredeom and dullness. Activities applying to dullness must be redefined well by you.

For instance, some dogs may typically have deleterious biting characters and will most likely be seen biting material, chair, mats, shoes and everything that they may see.

After governing out the teething problem if it's a pup, provide it with some massive sized playing balls and some mineral blend based bone materials.

You can also take your dog for a walk because walking can make your dog happy. It will also ensure that he will get enough exercise, promoting his health.

Playing with your dog is yet another way to prevent boredom. Play with him whenever you like or can. He can feel that playing and having fun is part of life, to and it would bring positive results in your training program because the dog will see that it is a daily routine.

You can also show some new tricks to your dog in order to prevent boredom and promote variety. In the process of your dog training you need to remember that it is important to establish and develop a two way communication with your dog. You will be in better tune with your dog. A better communication also makes it easier for your dog to learn more tricks.

You can also apply certain new tools to make things more interesting. There is the target stick and the clicker. Do not forget some treats because treats are the primary motivator and reinforcer for the dog to follow your commands.

Always remember that training your dog for new tricks is not just fun for you but for your dog as well. There are a lot of interesting new tricks that you can show your dog. You can beat boredom with teaching your dog tricks like to take a bow, shake a paw and to play dead. You can have lots of fun with your dog and boredom will never be a problem.

<u>Go Distraction Free:</u>

To achieve the most effective dog training results find a place that is calm and quiet. Your dog can easily be distracted. If you want to have his full attention, making this activity as stress free as possible, make sure that you are showing him your trick or task that you want him to perform in a place that is distraction-free.

Way 13: Toy Buying Tips

1. Try to buy a toy that matches your pet's size, not your size.

2. Make sure that there are no dangerous small pieces, as your pet could try to swallow it leading to choking, whereas if you tried to swallow it you just might feel really weird for the next three days.

3. Bones and sticks can splinter and cause choking and vomiting. Actually, they can even perforate your pet's mouth and throat (for those of you not in the know, perforating your throat is bad) so use non-splinter chew toys such as Nylabone Edible Bones, to allow your pet to gnaw with no fear.

4. Bells can be problematic for birds, besides just being really annoying. Use a treat dispensing roll toy instead, after all, food equals fun. On that note do not offer any leather toy (if not specially tanned), paint or any wood preservatives to your feathered friend for they can be toxic. So to recap, food equals fun, toxic equals not fun.

5. Cats often enjoy hiding out in plastic bags, and while you are unlikely to go to the pet store for the sole purpose of buying a plastic bag it is important to know because doing so can get their head stuck in it's handle, leading to choking and suffocation, so you're better off with a treat dispensing roll toy, which will not choke or suffocate them.

6. When purchasing toys online, make sure to do a price comparison before ordering because many online shops will offer seasonal discounts that you can cash in on.

ONCE YOU BOUGHT THE toy, make sure to supervise your dog while he or she plays with it in order to prevent accidents.

Way 14: First Steps In Grooming

Grooming is one of the important activities to be known well by the dog owner. If the dog owner is not aware of the grooming, then the dog may encounter many types of diseases. First steps of grooming consists of activities like maintenance of coat, nails and ears. The maintenance of the coat mainly consists of enrichment measures like proper bathing, combing, drying of skin by dryers, and more. The animal need not be bathed daily and this helps to protect the skin's characteristics like insulation feature.

Use conditioners and shampoos that are meant for dogs. Combing needs to be carried out with a soft brush meant for use in case of dogs. There are varieties of brushes available and depending on the type of breeds, one can use the concerned brush.

THIS GROOMING OF THE coat by a brush must be carried out daily and the fallen hair if any should be placed in a rubbish bin ASAP.

Never clip too much because this could well lead to wounds of nails.

Employ a sharpened clipper designed for dog clippin. It's much better to have the dog on the raised place and thus, the control over the animal is simpler. Ear canals are going to be checked up often and sterile cotton might be utilized for cleaning purposes.

Nail-maintenance is amongst the first steps of proper grooming activities. Nail areas can be simply clipped away and are always in light color. Do not touch the kind of red area of the nail in the higher position. Always have a strong grip if not, the dog will take a higher hand in the clipping and injury may happen.

Grooming your dog is very important for the dog itself. The dog feels more comfortable and this will have a more positive result in your training sessions. It is best that you do the grooming procedure on a regular basis. It is best to apply the grooming activity yourself since this grooming ritual would also bring you closer to your dog.

Way 15: Clipping A Dog

Many dog owners generally think of clipping as only a mechanical activity. Few understand that clipping a dog is an art. Clipping a coat or nail needs to be carried out in a careful manner to avoid the injuries to the skin or nail. Clipping of the coat is to be taken care of as per the breed characteristics. If the coat is not properly clipped, this may lead to the dust accumulation in the coat and the animal may start showing signs of skin diseases. This is true especially when the grooming activities are not done in a proper manner.

Clipping of coat helps to get rid of the parasitic burden to a greater extent and also, the clipping of your dog is of more useful to expose on the type of parasitic problem that the dog is likely to suffer. Many pet health parlors are available wherein the clipping of dog will be carried out in a more systematic manner.

CLIPPING OF COAT HELPS to eliminate the parasitic burden to a very great extent and additionally, the clipping of your dog is of more handy to reveal on the sort of parasitic problem the dog is probably going to suffer.

Many pet health parlors are available whereby the clipping of dog will be carried out in a methodical demeanour. Always utilize a sharpened clipper and in winter regions, avoid the close clipping. That is due to the undeniable fact that the closer clipping in winter seasons may expose the dog to the environmental strains like the cold climate.

Hence, the dog may become more vulnerable to the frostbite. Avoid the close clipping of coat or nail because this may cause injury to the underlying tissues and may cause bleeding in the concerned animal.

Many pet owners need to avoid any clipping activity when the animal is not in healthy status. Clipping instruments are available to a greater extent in many pet shops. Avoid the blunt instruments because they may not clip well and hence, repetition is required often. Always use modern equipments for clipping activities.

. . ⚓ . .

AN ESSENTIAL PART OF pet grooming is the trimming of your pet's nails. If your pet shows any sign of pain stop, what you're doing and comfort your dog.

Most dogs actually do not like pet grooming and the ordeal of nail trimming can be a very a stressful times for your dog. Gently put the nail into the opening of the nail trimmers and slowly but firmly clip the nail.

Avoid the close clipping of coat or nail because this could lead to injury to the fundamental tissues and may lead to bleeding, too.

Many animal owners need to avoid any clipping activity when the animal isn't in a very healthy standing.

Clipping instruments are available to a more serious extent in several pet shops.

Avoid the blunt instruments because they may not clip well and thus, repetition is needed frequently.

Always use modern and the latest equipments for clipping your dog.

Professional pet groomers on the other hand are a little more experienced and they clip the nails at a faster rate than the novice nail clipper.

If you do happen to cut the blood vessel, grab a clean cloth or sanitary paper towel to put pressure on the nail until the bleeding stops.

This method is very stressful for the animal and nail clipping might be a horrible experience for your dog.

Way 16: Bathing A Dog & Home Spa

Bathing a dog needs to be given more emphasis. This is because of the fact that if you are careless in bathing, the animal may end up having some infections. For example, if you don't close the ears with large cotton ball, the water may enter into ear canals and may cause some ear infections with signs like constant discharge from the ears and shaking of head.

Frequency of bathing actually depends on the breed of the dog. If the dog is of a hairy type like the cocker spaniel, then the bathing is to be carried out once in six to eight weeks. If these breeds are bathed too frequently, then the skin and coat loose the protective characters. However, when the dog has defecated on the skin due to the frequent digestive upsets leading to diarrhea, to avoid the bad smell, the dog may be subjected to frequent bathing some times by the owners.

Take more care in avoiding some irritant soaps or human soaps. The soap materials used for human beings are not suitable for dogs. Similarly, many human shampoo products are having some ingredients that are not suitable in the proportions that are to be used in case of dogs. Hence, always try to use the shampoo products that are mentioned mainly for use in dogs. Take more care in using any new product.

TRY AND HAVE A LEASH, conditioner, towel, and shampoo in a handy place. Conditioner is useful to make the brushing activity simpler later on. Washing should be a convenient activity to both the dog and the owner.

This shouldn't be a burden, but a fun activity!

Way 17: Everything You Have To Know About Dog Identification & Dog Microchipping

> Pet identification is highly required in these days because of the need for the licensing of the dog in a proper manner and to reduce the numbers of the stray dog menace in streets. Pet identification is done by many methods, which are different from each other. The cost factor for that also has variations accordingly.
>
> The identification of your pet may be done by personalized tags, sometimes by the municipal license tag, rabies tag, and more. Most of the time, your telephone number and your name will be on a place in the personalized tags of the dogs. If anybody encounters the dog accidentally during the event of missing of the dog will become capable of reporting the facts to the concerned officials.
>
> Plastic and metal pet identification tags are available in multiple colors and the dog owners can choose the color they want. However, many select the reflective type of dog tags along with the collars. Hence, the dogs can be identified even in darkness to a greater extent.

IDEALLY, IMPLEMENT at least two methods to ensure a safe return should your dog get lost or missing.

Microchips and tatoos provide permanent ways to identify a dog. You will need to list your dog with one of the many tattoo registry programs around the country.

Luckily, dog ID tags are not expensive to buy, so it should be one of the first things you purchase for your dog, once you've chosen a name for your pet. Just a few minutes of your time to update registry info or purchase a new dog tag can make all the difference in the world.

Microchips are minuscule electronic chips that are embedded under your dog's skin.

Recently many electronic contraptions are available like microchips which are inserted into the dog. But these sorts of electronic chips have to be implanted behind the ears and once implanted, this can help trace the dog electronically.

A collard and tagged animal shows that it's not a stray animal and this gives more security to the dog and tracing the missed animal will become simpler for the animal owners typically because of the identification-based dog collars.

Dog tags can easily be removed, but it would take a difficult surgical procedure to remove a microchip.

A microchip is no bigger than a grain of rice, and veterinarians can implant the chips into all kinds of dogs.

AVID claims that its microchips help reunite as many as 1,400 pets with their owners every day, and HomeAgain touts a growing total of more than 400,000 pet recoveries [source: AVID, HomeAgain].

Either way will guarantee a secure life for your beloved dog.

Dog Health Quiz

ALL YOU HAVE TO DO is find 12 Healthy Dog's Lifestyle related words. Use your imagination, read backwards, sideways, and forwards to find the correct dog related words and associations. Go to the next page to see the correct answers!

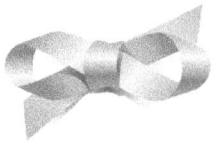

Have fun:)

Answers

1. Breeds
2. Nutrition
3. Breeding
4. Foods
5. Treats
6. Vitamins
7. Obesity
8. Sterilization
9. Mating
10. Spraying
11. Neutering
12. Supplements

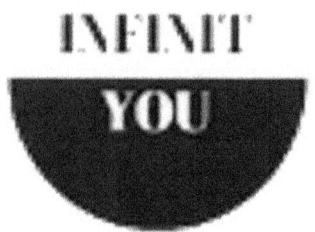

About the Publisher

InfinitYou is a hybrid general interest trade publisher. One of the first of its kind InfinitYou publishes physical books, electronic books, and audiobooks in various genres. Our publications are meant to educate, edify and entertain readers of all walks of life from babies to the elderly. Home to more than twenty imprints such as Infinit Baby, Infinit Kids, Infinit Girl, Infinit Boy, Infinit Coloring, Infinit Swear Words, Infinit Activities, Infinit Productivity, Infinit Cat, Infinit Dog, Infinit Love, Infinit Family, Infinit Survival, Infinit Health, Infinit Beauty, Infinit Spirituality, Infinit Lifestyle, Infinit Wealth, Infinit Romance, and lots more.

www.ingramcontent.com/pod-product-compliance
Lightning Source LLC
LaVergne TN
LVHW020443080526
838202LV00055B/5325